MW00608349

I Am Too Blessed to Be Broke:

Breaking the Curse of Poverty Mindset in the Church

Copyright © 2021 by **Shavonna Perkins** All rights reserved Published by beyondthebookmedia.com All rights reserved. No part of this publication may be reproduced, distributed, or transmitted in any form or by any means, including photocopying, recording, or other electronic or mechanical methods, without the prior written permission of the publisher, except in the case of brief quotations embodied in critical reviews and certain other noncommercial uses permitted by copyright law. For permission requests, write to the publisher, addressed "Attention: Permissions Coordinator," at the address below. Limit of Liability/Disclaimer of Warranty: While the publisher and author have used their best efforts in preparing this book, they make no representations of warranties with respect to the accuracy or completeness of the contents of this book and specifically disclaim any implied warranties or merchantability or fitness for a particular purpose. No warranty may be created or extended by sales representatives or written sales materials. The advice and strategies contained herein may not be suitable for your situation. You should consult with a professional where appropriate. Neither the publisher nor author shall be liable for damages arising here from. Beyond The Book Media, LLC Alpharetta. GA www.beyondthebookmedia.com The publisher is not responsible for websites that are not owned by the publisher. **ISBN: 978-1-953788-38-2 (Printed)**

Shavonna Perkins

I Am Too Blessed to Be Broke:

Breaking the Curse of Poverty Mindset in the Church

Dedication

To my husband and my children, you all are my biggest cheerleaders. You understand the sacrifices that must be made but are also willing to jump in the fire with me. Thank you to my loving husband, who made sure that I had nothing to worry about nightly for 21 days while writing this book.

To my mother, if only I could be as strong as the woman that you are. Thank you for the many sacrifices you make for us to be successful.

To my father, thank you for always believing in me. I can remember some of your last words to me. "You're doing a great job." You supported your children in everything we put our hands on. I know you would be so proud of all we've accomplished; until we meet again.

To my Pastor, family, friends, and hometown of Bertie, thank you for molding, shaping, encouraging, and believing me.

TABLE OF CONTENTS

INTRODUCTION **9**

CHAPTER 1: THIS IS FOR YOU 13

CHAPTER 2: LET'S TALK ABOUT IT 23

CHAPTER 3: I AM WEALTHY.
IT'S A MINDSET THING 35

CHAPTER 4: STRATEGIC STEWARDSHIP 51

CHAPTER 5: OUR RESPONSIBILITY TO GOD 59

CHAPTER 6: THE BORROWER VS. THE LENDER 71

CHAPTER 7: MANAGING YOUR MONEY GODS WAY 87

APPENDIX **107**

INTRODUCTION

I can only imagine what you're thinking; here's another person who feels the need to coach me on how to manage MY money. You're also probably thinking since I am a financial coach looking to teach you, I must come from wealth, right? I must have years of experience dating back to when I was an adolescent; seeing and having all the best examples displayed growing up? Better yet, it's easy for someone who "seems" to have money to know how to handle it, right? I hate to disappoint you. However, none of this could be further from the truth.

I'll let you in on a secret; I didn't fully comprehend the relationship between humanity and money until recently, let alone God and money. But wait, before spilling all my tea, why am I writing this book? Why did God speak to me about the importance of this book, and more specifically, now? One morning at 4:00am, God woke me up to give me this simple formula:

The lack of knowledge + the mindset of lack = generations living outside of the promises of God.

Sadly, one of the most baffling issues attacking the Christian community is whether God wants us to be wealthy. Do we not think God wants us to have his best? The lack of knowledge around this question will cause many of us to miss out on our blessings. Not understanding God's will for our lives places us outside of the position for God to bless us or His favor to overflow in our lives.

Why is it easier for us to yell we're broke than to declare we're wealthy? We access things stored up by faith, and everything we need is already available; we must be in a position to accept it. 2 Corinthians 9:8 tells us that God can pour on our blessings in astonishing ways so that we're prepared for anything and everything, more than just ready to do what needs to be done.

The spirit of lack comes from people who do not operate in their spirit of authority. I'll let you in on a secret; money doesn't take the place of salvation. You can be saved and have more than enough. Appreciating and wanting nice things doesn't mean that you're worldly; you can be holy and look nice! As Christians, we need to change our mindset about living our best and desired lifestyle. God doesn't want us forgoing luxury nor ashamed of his blessings because we're confessing to be Christians. The devil is a liar!

This will be my first time saying this aloud, but I will no longer walk around a timid, blessed Christian. I am letting the world know that I am a Christian living in a nice neighborhood, who likes driving nice cars and wearing nice things, whether Target, Gucci, Louis Vuitton, or Christian Louboutin, and I pay my tithes and bills monthly. Your nice thing, perhaps, is a boat, a one-of-a-kind pen, or the winning ball from the 2016 World Series Championship Game. No matter what that is for you, understand that you can ask God for nice things and have salvation.

This book is for those looking to manage their finances God's way, break generational curses, and change their mindset about living their best life. Even if you didn't come from wealth or see wealth growing up, this is for you if you want and desire to do better. There is a way to live wealthy, righteous, and most importantly, manage your finances Gods way. So, keep reading! Besides, you're too blessed to be broke.

CHAPTER 1: THIS IS FOR YOU

So, I recommend having fun because there is nothing better for people in this world than eating, drinking, and enjoying life. That way, they will experience some happiness along with all the hard work God gives them under the sun.

-ECCLESIASTES 8:15 (NLT)

"Baby, unfortunately, mommy and daddy don't have it right now. We'll have to wait until payday" are the words that close to 70% of our households with children hear; for just a simple request such as food, toiletries, or even a new pair of socks. As heartbreaking as it can be for both the child and parent, I've heard this statement a few times, and it is the reality of those families living paycheck to paycheck.

If I must be honest, my journey with money has been a rollercoaster. Growing up, I felt my family was sometimes in survival mode. Let's take it back to the late 80s, early 90s. As a young girl born in Bridgeport, CT, who later moved to NC, I've been in church since the womb (literally). I was one of those kids where the church was all I knew, yet my parents managed to raise us in a balanced household (thank you, God). I promise my reasoning for telling you this will make sense by the end of this chapter.

My father was in his 20s when he started to suffer from multiple heart attacks making him unable to work. In turn, this forced him to go on disability at a very early age. With my father being on disability, my mother was the sole breadwinner of the home, requiring us to live on a limited income.

Growing up in a small town was interesting, but growing up in Bertie County, listed in 2019 as the poorest county in North Carolina (out of 100), came with additional challenges. Challenges that were unavoidable when the 2019 median household income was just a little over $35,000. A county where over 60% of the population is African American and 25% live below the poverty line. Significantly higher than the national average of 12.3%, according to datausa.io. Don't get me wrong; everyone wasn't broke, busted, and disgusted.

I would put everyone into three categories: 1) You had more than enough required for your environment and was doing just fine; 2) You managed with what was available to you but had a desire for more, or simply put, 3) You didn't have it and lived every day on a wing and a prayer; unfortunately, most of the population falling into the last two categories. So, one can imagine my experiences growing up and how I saw wealth.

Most of what I witnessed of true wealth to be was through what I saw on TV. People lived paycheck to paycheck, most times not knowing the source of their next dollar. Sadly, to say, their paycheck, once received, was needed to pay back someone else, ultimately falling into this never-ending cycle of working, paying back the last person, and borrowing again from a different person until the next payday. It was very natural for most people to work at the local lumber or chicken factory, at that time barely making $8 an hour. Yet, I always felt safe and secure because of my parents.

My fondest elementary school memory and probably what taught me to appreciate and value money was finding coins around the house to take to the bank. Exchanging the rolled coins would either be used for a special treat from Tastee-Freeze or carry the family until the next payday. Back then, we only ate out on Fridays, or if the third of the month, disability check fell during the week. Of course, it isn't like that today, and if I must be honest, in today's time, sometimes it's just convenient to pick up the kid's food during the week; and depending on how busy the week is, multiple times during the week. My siblings and I received a lot of our wants and had a fantastic childhood, but, until this day, I'm not sure at what cost.

I only missed one trip in all my K-12 years. I remember it like it was yesterday. In 8th grade, we went to the Spirit of Norfolk, a yacht located in downtown Norfolk, VA, offering lunch and dinner cruises. I remember they asked us to dress up, and boy was I excited; I'm sure as soon as Mrs. Bowen and Mr. Warren told us, I had already picked out my go-to outfit, which was black slacks, a floral top, and my black leather chunky platform shoes. I never thought I would use the word platform and feel as "mature" as my parents' generation.

The trip was around $40, but when I asked my parents, they regretfully informed me they didn't have it, and I had to stay back at school with a few other kids. Unfortunately, there was a short period between permission slips going out and the trip itself. Now that I think back, I'm like, oh my, it was only $40. Just this past summer, we spent $135/week on camp for my son. However, I took it like a champ. Hence the reason I started working at the age of 16. As my parents took care of our needs, I wanted to take the weight of my wants off them.

Additionally, with my father having heart complications with multiple procedures and surgeries during my childhood, my goal was never to be an extra burden. He loved his kids so much, when he couldn't provide even the least bit, it worried him. However, best believe this was the last and only trip I missed, thanks to my parents. As time progressed and my parents started to add more income into the household, they had a bit more wiggle room in their finances through cleaning jobs and contracts with local banks. Part of me wanted to make sure they enjoyed the extra money and did things they enjoyed. Don't get me wrong, I was 16 at the time, a massive saver, meaning I held tight to at least half of every dollar I received, so I would still lean on my parents for support.

Even when it was time to go to college, I deposited my graduation money into my Wachovia (now Wells Fargo) bank account. I went to Wal-Mart to put everything I needed for college on layaway. When I told my parents, they were shocked and insisted they pay the final total and all the remaining items required to attend college. I had an older sister who went off to college and attended NC A&T four years ahead of me, so I took note of everything I needed and kept that mental note until it was time for me to graduate; and again, I wanted to put the least amount of stress on my parents. I've always told my husband my independence and managing money started at a young age.

I often noticed that it seemed like those in the church were the ones who lived paycheck to paycheck or had to constantly "rob Peter to pay Paul" (that's an old saying). I somewhat understood the concept of paying tithes and offerings at a young age, as I would receive monetary gifts for my birthday or holidays and would make sure I set aside a few dollars for God. But I remember at times questioning why my family was in certain situations if they paid their tithes and offering. I had to remember that lessons on money management weren't available.

As an adult and looking at things comprehensively, I now understand that not only did my family income play a part, but it was also the lack of knowledge and the environment where we lived. I often wonder why there wasn't anyone, just one person around, to teach others about better financial freedom. Whether this was someone in or outside of the church, where were they? In God's greatness, now fifteen years later, I realized I was looking for me.

As I made my way through life and received encouragement from my parents, family, teachers, and those around me, I realized that I wanted more financial stability for my family and me. Not only did I have to learn to manage money better, but I had to undergo mindset and lifestyle shifts to bring me to the point of being financially secured today.

On my quest for financial wellness, I received a degree in Accounting from NC State University and began my journey. Good money management over the years has afforded my husband and me our dream wedding, a lovely home, investment properties, businesses, and the ability to raise two kids comfortably with money set aside for both the nice to have and emergencies. Don't get me wrong, it hasn't been a cakewalk, more like a crate walk. For a very accurate picture, google the 2021 crate walk challenge; enough said.

We've experienced the loss of jobs, not once but twice, the decline in income once receiving a job, and everything that comes with losing a job. However, through the grace and wisdom of God, we had a plan (i.e., budget) in place that allowed us not to miss a beat and pay off bills using money in savings. My goal is to help educate the almost 70% of people out there living paycheck to paycheck. No matter where you come from, hopefully, this book will put you on the right track for managing your money, thus teaching your kids and family how to manage their finances effectively. Please repeat after me; we're breaking generational curses in Jesus' name.

The Importance of Financial Literacy

Being that close to 70% of Americans are in debt, the time is now to discuss the importance of financial literacy. Financial literacy is just a big word to describe the foundation of your relationship with money and the use of fundamental financial skills to make mature financial decisions. When you're financially literate, you can better prepare yourself for two essential things that affect everyone: what you know is coming and what you don't know is coming.

You are ultimately being prepared for the attainable and positioned for the unforeseeable financial situations of life. There is a strong correlation between confidence and money management. Once you understand your finances, you will confidently manage your finances and give, ultimately receiving more. Do you see the pattern here and how it comes full circle? You manage, give, get, manage, give, and get. The Bible tells us that if you're giving, you will get. Most of us understand this concept through the biblical principle of sowing and reaping. But you will never understand the potential magnitude of your giving until you've learned to manage. So why is financial literacy important? Why do we discuss finances?

- Until Jesus is first in our finances, Jesus isn't first in our life.
- Whether we want to believe it or not, money rules the land.
- How we use our money is a form of worship to God
- Discussing finances is the source of financial freedom
- Racial Wealth Gap
- For couples, money issues are the leading cause of divorce.
- For parents, the more you talk about money and the responsibility of it; the more your kids will know

As the Founder of The Bougie Wealth Group™, I am a mother, wife, sister, and friend. Most importantly, as a Certified Financial Education Instructor, I am gifted to help others win and succeed financially. With over 15 years of experience in the financial industry, consulting, coaching and training, I help others obtain financial freedom by changing their mindset and attaining their desired lifestyle. You may not be, but I am still in awe. Who would've imagined, Financial Instructor who grew up in one of the poorest counties in NC, helping others on their financial journey to wealth and living their desired lifestyle?

The realization is, God didn't place us on this earth to work, live in lack, and die broke. Although our ultimate reward is in heaven, earthly treasures were still created with us in mind. Treasures to enjoy while living our day-to-day lives (Ecclesiastes 8:15). God wants us to enjoy life now, knowing that an even better reward is coming. I remember the days as a child when it was my birthday. I would have a party or cupcakes at school, and I was happy. But knowing later, my mom was driving my friends and me to the mall to Claire's was the icing on top. That made me want to enjoy the present time at school with classmates and cupcakes, even more, knowing that the fun was only beginning.

CHAPTER 2: LET'S TALK ABOUT IT

By doing this, they will be storing up their treasure as a good foundation for the future so that they may experience true life.
1 TIMOTHY 6:19 (NLT)

Growing up, for most of us, money being talked about or managed was either a good or bad experience. Our financial decisions have stemmed from what we saw growing up, no matter our influence. I saw an article circulating the internet of two brothers, one in business attire and successful and one homeless and struggling as a drunk. When asked why they chose their lifestyle, they both responded with the same answer, "my father was an alcoholic." Ultimately, it's our choice to decide which route we'll take.

As you read in the introduction and first chapter, the effect of my childhood and, at times living paycheck to paycheck influenced me to manage my money wisely and made talking about money with my spouse a top priority. My husband and I have monthly budget meetings making it a priority in our marriage, thus limiting (keyword limiting, not avoiding) disagreements about our finances.

For me, my childhood influenced me to make a change and to change my mindset. Use your experiences to shape your financial journey as well. Until you're able to get past any hurt, resentment, or lousy behavior modeled as standard, you will never free yourself to live in your purpose. I hear the Holy Spirit saying that many people often stay stuck because of what momma or grandma did. What is God telling you to do? How is the Holy Spirit convicting you about how you manage your money?

Most people see finances as one of the most challenging topics over politics, religion, and even death. With money issues being the leading cause of divorce and stress, you would think it would be discussed and taught more. When we do not talk about money, we open ourselves up to issues in our family, relationships and even continue to or find ourselves starting generational curses. Somewhere along the line, there was a rule of thumb that stated that you do not mention your pay, money, or finances. According to theatlantic.com, 34% of couples can't identify how much money their spouse makes. People feel more comfortable talking with friends about marital discord, mental health, addiction, race, and politics than financial security.

Unfortunately, church leaders have a hard time discussing finances and the importance of financial literacy in their congregation. Talking about finances or money can be confused with only needing it for self-greed. Many we observe stand in that sacred office and abuse and misuse their title, leaving many congregants confused, destitute, and questioning God's will for their lives.

When we begin to understand that the proper terms for giving money to the church are tithes and offering, and truly understand the meaning and principles of those terms, it will make it easier to understand financial management and giving. However, we can't talk about tithe and offering if we don't talk about money management. Yes, there are times when we must make faith moves whether the money is there or not, but having to make a decision every week or month on whether you're going to give to God or pay your utility bills isn't of God as my mom would say. Yet, we continue to brush this subject under the rug. God doesn't desire us to live in lack or ignorance.

Pastor Sarah Jakes Roberts mentioned while preaching, "God doesn't set expectations where there is no ability." God isn't expecting anything from us that we can't fulfill. Nor is He telling us to manage our money and be good stewards if He doesn't think we can do so. Although we may not see it, God sees our potential.

According to VancoFaith, only 1.5 million people out of the 247 million people identified as Christians pay their tithes. When our preachers and evangelicals fail to teach on personal finances, they fail to preach the whole gospel and council of God. Unfortunately, we often fail to talk about finances in church (aside from tithing and offering) because financial literacy and stewardship must start from the top. If the pastor isn't managing their finances correctly, he can't preach or teach his congregation about managing money.

According to www.churchleadership.com, many clergies feel awkward in those moments and find it challenging to lead in this realm. Often, it is because they haven't had these conversations within their own families and have not acquired the skills or habits of sound personal finance. The article alluded to the burdens preacher carry from the residual impact of professional education or other debts.

If our preachers do not have basic financial and economic literacy, they aren't credible when discussing God's economy.

They should feel as confident speaking to a member about money management as they are visiting them in the hospital. Our preachers should have something to offer to the many in their congregations who live in quiet financial desperation, and they should be prepared to talk both about the burdens of poverty and its causes.

Close to 70% of Americans are in debt, and they should be preaching, teaching, and modeling a debt-free life. Sadly, money is one of the most significant spiritual challenges facing the people of the church. How dare the church and place of healing not talk and teach their parishioners practical ways to manage money and recover from financial losses and disparities. So, in case you can't tell, I am adamant about us talking about personal finances in the church, and this is a discussion that should've started yesterday.

What Is Money & Why Is It Needed?

Do we really understand what money is and why it's needed? You must be thinking, duh, I know what money is! My mortgage, rent, kids, and self-care needs can tell you why it's needed. According to Positive Money, money is any object accepted as payment for goods and services or repayment of debts in each country or socio-economic context. Money is a medium of exchange, a unit of account, a store of value. And all those items you mentioned were indeed correct. In essence, money is the source of goods needed for survival.

Think about it. Everything you have comes with a cost. That includes your living arrangements, whether buying or renting, clothes, and food. Even if you're a gardener, someone had to pay for the initial seed. Think about it and look around you. Name one thing that didn't cost you or someone else? Even this book you're reading came at a cost. Whether you feel like you'll never have enough or have a love-hate relationship with it, money is an essential tool God has given us to fulfill his promises and purpose in our lives.

The only way you can say you lived a day without any costly goods or services is to sleep in the woods, hunting for your food and making your bed and clothes out of leaves and bark. Yep, living in the natural, only off things created by God. Do you see the correlation here and why money rules the land? Thus, is the number one area that affects God's people the hardest and sometimes most uncomfortable matter to discuss.

You may say, well, I like free stuff. As my grandma would always say, "Baby, the only thing free in this world is salvation." And now, understanding the meaning of money and its importance puts the reality of this statement into perspective. No matter how much money you have, you can't buy your way into heaven! Aren't you glad you serve a God who isn't like unto man, determining eternal life for you by the one thing the world uses to determine your status?

If knowing this isn't enough to make you want to serve God with everything in your heart AND do all you can to manage your finances His way, I'm not for sure what else it'll take. Besides needing money for the barest necessities of life, money also helps us live and achieve our desired goals. Christian or not, I don't know anyone who would agree that money isn't needed, let alone necessary. The question resides, where is your faith? In God or your money? Maybe that is where some of us have gone wrong.

What Does God Say About Money?

What exactly does God say about money? Is it even mentioned in the Bible? Well, I'm glad you asked. Money is a term used in the Bible over 800 times! Not 8! Not 80! Not 500! Over 800 times is money mentioned in the Bible. That seems rather important. Well, the reality is, it is. Understanding the importance of money and knowing that God talks about it multiple times in the most incredible instruction manual for humanity is pretty amazing. Our job as great stewards and disciples is to manage our finances in God's way, to understand the fundamental importance of money and the correct way to use it to live our desired lifestyle as close to the will of God as possible.

So, is money bad? A question that a lot of people ponder, especially Christians. God has given us life and life more abundantly. That includes being able to enjoy life and the things available to us. So why wouldn't money be included in that since the material things available to us require money? Isn't money the one thing that fuels this world? Isn't money the one thing everyone needs no matter age, race, nationality, religion, or sex?

When carrying our children, my husband and I would joke how the first thing we give babies when born is a hospital record and a medical charge. Of course, we know some of it is taken care of by insurance, but even before they have a name, the doctor recommends their first shot, and their billing record begins. So as soon as conception occurs, money or the responsibility around money is attached to us.

Inherently, money isn't good or bad; more so, people's actions when using money make it appear good or bad.

When we fail to realize that all gifts and resources are from God's grace and generosity, we then enter the danger zone, the red zone I like to call it. 1 Timothy 6:10 states that money is the root of all evil, right? Is that correct? NO. The Bible says that the LOVE of money is the root of all evil. God specifically tells us in his word to be great stewards over the money He gives us (Matthew 25:14-27). So why would money be considered evil?

Jesus also tells us that wealth can be dangerous. Ultimately money isn't bad; again, it's the fixation over money that pushes us into the red zone. In Mark 10:23-27, "Jesus looked around and said to his disciples, "How hard it is for the rich to enter the kingdom of God. The disciples were amazed at his words. But Jesus said again, "Children, how hard it is to enter the kingdom of God! It is easier for a camel to go through the eye of a needle than for someone rich to enter the kingdom of God. The disciples were even more amazed and said to each other, "Who then can be saved? Jesus looked at them and said, "With man, this is impossible, but not with God; all things are possible with God." How you view money has a lot to do with your action towards it.

We must remember that at the end of the day, money can't buy complete happiness. The keyword here is complete, as money can provide a level of unmeasured happiness to someone homeless. It can provide earthly joy and open the door for options. It can potentially make you happy for a given period, but once it's gone, we sometimes find that our joy leaves with it. What brings long-term satisfaction and contentment can only be found in Jesus. So that means that even when the money has run out, God is still good, and you still have joy. It is not the idea of wealth or riches itself that makes it evil.

Some great things can be accomplished with money when used correctly. The story of the Good Samaritan found in Luke 10:25-37 is a perfect example. Other examples include reputable and trustworthy charitable organizations that build houses, feed and clothe the poor.

There isn't anywhere where it states that you're automatically destined for hell if you're wealthy. Instead, the devotion to wealth and money is incompatible with a relationship with God. You can't serve both God and your bank account. You can't serve God and somehow fail to commune with Him because you're always working. Some people must work on Sundays to make a living for their family; however, everyone doesn't need to work every Sunday. Again, we begin to enter the red zone when it seems like we're working every day and putting money and our employment before our relationship with God. God is required and must always be the essential thing in our lives. (Luke 16:13).

Above all, your greatest goal should be serving others, laying your foundation, and attaining riches in heaven. When you make serving God your greatest goal, you already have access to the most incredible means (Timothy 6:19). Sometimes we get so caught up in making or chasing the dollar that we forget about the provider.

Can I Be a Wealthy Christian?

Can you be a wealthy Christian? Is that an oxymoron? We've been groomed to think being close to God means being poor. Others feel that you've jeopardized your relationship with God, done something illegal or unchristian like to attain wealth. Well, you can stop holding your breath. You are not going to hell for being wealthy or desiring nice things. God isn't pleased with us living below our privileges and below what He has for us. Gods' wealth is available to us, and He doesn't want us to dwell in poverty.

Janice Bryant Howroyd said it best, "the gift of great work is great wealth." The most significant knowledge you can have in this world is that of the almighty God, knowing God and that God loves us and is concerned about us. What does it look like for God to save us, and we live in misery? In the richness of his grace, God has made available to us all his goodness to enjoy.

The Bible tells us that the wealth of the wicked is laid up for the righteous, correct? The Apostle Paul admonishes us to remember that the world's riches are only for the present; this shouldn't be the source of our hope. Be generous and use them for good works. So, God, you're saying the only requirement to being wealthy is to keep you at the source, promise to be generous, and help those who don't have? Sign me up; you no longer need to read anymore! The secret is out!!! You may be saying, but if only it were that simple.

My pastor, James P. Perkins Sr., motto is you get more when you give more, so maybe it's just that simple. You can be wealthy and a Christian; you can't worship God and worship your riches. Because God gives us free will, money, unfortunately, has been a tool that has disconnected so many from the will and promises of God. It is great to have a relationship with money and your finances to understand how you should budget, save, and give; however, it is even better to have a relationship with God, who has cattle on a thousand hills. God tells us in Psalms 50:10, "for every animal of the forest is mine, and the cattle on a thousand hills. I know every bird in the mountains, and the creatures of the field are mine. If I were hungry, I would not tell you, for the world is mine, and all that is in it."

Ultimately EVERYTHING belongs to God. Please take this time to hear what I'm saying. EVERYTHING, literally E-V-E-R-Y-T-H-I-N-G, belongs to God, meaning He has imminent domain, so why do we worry? We find in Psalms 24:1 that the earth is the Lord's, and everything in it, the world, and all who live in it. So why do we feel like we can have wealth and riches without God? Now that's an oxymoron.

Our son Logan often jokes and says, "Mommy and Daddy, this is my house, and I'm never leaving; I'll let you stay here, though." As a 5-year-old, that's pretty funny; but as the parents whose name is on the mortgage and deed, that statement wouldn't stand in the court of law. Saying you're wealthy and having money in the bank without having a relationship with God is pretty much the same thing; you're taking ownership over something that doesn't even belong to you. Everything you possess, it was God's before you got it.

My pastor once said, every blessing comes from the hand of God and originated by the hand of God. Once we begin to love God and God's people over money, we will understand the relationship of money in our lives. There is only one source of true wealth, only one promising means of lasting security, and that is being in Christ. Let's learn to put God's promises, people, and purpose over profit, then will we happily and securely enjoy the wealth God has placed in our lives.

CHAPTER 3: I AM WEALTHY.
IT'S A MINDSET THING

When doubts filled my mind, your comfort gave me renewed
hope and cheer.

-PSALMS 94:19 (NLT)

To be in the place that I am now ultimately required a shift in my mind. I had to get past what I saw growing up and realize that it didn't have to define me. Undergoing mindset changes aren't easy, but it's worth it, and as you've read, I know from experience. There were times where honestly, it felt easier to want to give up because I felt safe in what I knew rather than the unknown. I had to trust God's will over my why. Sometimes we stay in a posture of disobedience because we believe we are safer, which is the ultimate definition of fear. I've personally stayed in positions longer than I was supposed to because I didn't feel safe in the unknown. It starts with changing your mindset because your mind is the playground for fear.

Our relationships or environments can influence fear. When we operate in the spirit of fear, mentally, we immediately become in defense or avoidance mode. As I sat in my college accounting classes, I became fearful, feeling underqualified compared to my peers. I realized that they'd come from a wealthy family or environment where they already knew what I had to learn, starting at the basics. Aren't I glad in those moments I prayed for the renewal of my mind, a mindset to see it to the end? December 19, 2009, at 9:00 am, sitting in what was the RBC Center with my cap and gown on, I understood God's will over my why and why I couldn't give up. I had an entire family and community waiting on me to help them elevate their mindset.

A Renewed Mind: Required for Change

Before starting a successful weight loss journey, one must determine that losing weight is achievable. Mentally, one must be able to see themselves at the finish line. We often word-curse ourselves before starting by saying, "well, I don't know why I'm doing this; it's not like it's going to work." At this point, defeat has taken its crown of victory before you've gotten started, simply because our words have power, which is the very opposite of having faith. Last I checked, faith is the substance of things hoped for, the evidence of things not seen. It's no different as we begin to start our financial journey.

Think about this question: what have you purposed in your mind that you'll never be able to afford? When you do not comprehend the possibility of being wealthy, your mind will never figure out how to build wealth. To renew your mind is to replace old thinking with new thinking and free yourself from generational curses, bondage, and brokenness.

Maybe you've seen a parent only pay half the bill or called month after month to get an extension on their account. Those are generational curses that may seem like it's an okay or normal thing to do. Until you change your mindset to say, I will pay my bills on time and in full; you will never free yourself from that area of bondage. The Bible tells us in Romans 12:2, "do not conform to the pattern of this world but be transformed by the renewing of your mind. Then you will be able to test and approve what God's will is—his good, pleasing and perfect will." The renewing of one's mind requires control and authority. As a man thinketh, so is he (Proverbs 23:7). So, if you think you're broke, you will most likely be broke; if you think you're sick, you will most likely become sick. The power of your words shapes the outcome of your lifestyle.

I remember leaving the house during the 2020 pandemic. Whenever I would return and happen to see an article or hear the news about a newly discovered symptom, I would immediately (and naturally) think, "Is that something I've experienced?" More times than not, because I thought maybe I had that symptom the week before, I would immediately feel it again and go into a slight panic until I would tell myself I was okay. Suddenly, I would forget, move on to something else, and somehow, that symptom I "thought" I had, I no longer felt. What am I trying to say here? Because for a second, I thought about it, trying to figure out if I had it or not, that is what I became, and unfortunately, if I allowed myself to stay in that posture, it would've been detrimental.

Your mindset is one of the essential things required for healthy self-esteem. Two types of mindsets, made popular by Carol Dweck in her book Mindset: The New Psychology of Success, was fixed and growth mindsets. With a Fixed Mindset, people believe their character and attributes are set and cannot be changed. They most likely fear that they aren't talented or smart enough to achieve their goals, so when faced with obstacles, they give up easily.

Ultimately, they don't believe they can improve, so naturally, they don't try. Contrary, with a Growth Mindset, people think they can grow and develop with effort, drive, and consistency with time. When faced with obstacles, they persist in setbacks and see effort as the path to mastery. In the long run, thorough trying, effort, and persistence give them a greater sense of free will.

While on this financial journey, it's imperative to have a growth mindset. If you continue, you will never end where you started. There will be challenges and setbacks, unexpected expenses, and times where it seems like you had more money before you began taking control of your finances. It will be a requirement to see your effort as one of the most excellent solutions in your journey to wealth.

Changing your mindset about money will change how and when you spend your money, leading to better choices. How you think about money will determine your actions towards money. When mindset changes happen, and you think positively about your money, whether you have $100 in debt or $10,000 in debt, your attitude is always focused on the solution. You have two choices; to analyze what can be done to pay it off or automatically think and assume that you will forever be in debt. As you can see, your mentality has a lot to do with how you manage your finances.

We must take authority over the debt and poverty mindset and speak life. It's a sad commentary (as my pastor would say) when we can speak life over our health, children, or things we desire but can't speak life over our finances or debt we've incurred. You have not because you ask not. My God can do exceedingly abundantly above all that I can ask or think (Ephesians 3:20), and I choose to hold Him to his word. Malachi 3:10 says, "Bring ye the whole tithe into the storehouse, that there may be food in my house, and prove me now herewith, saith Jehovah of hosts, if I will not open you the windows of heaven, and pour you out a blessing, that there shall not be room enough to receive it."

I'm a little competitive (shh, don't tell anyone), but all I needed to see was "prove me now." Bet, God checkmate (not literally), I'm ready. But also at ease knowing that God always wins, which means I will always win. And you know what I love most about this scripture is the simplicity. God didn't come with a long list of instructions or GPS turns; make a left, then make a right, then make a U-turn, merge to the left, get in the right lane, and maybe your destination is on the right. I'm ready for my outpour, and I'm prepared to receive. But again, it starts in your heart and leads to your mind. Spiritual discipline goes hand and hand with financial discipline.

Poverty Mindset

Living in the idea of just enough is an insult to God. It is equivalent to saying that I am safe, barely making it to heaven, forgetting about winning souls for Christ, or performing works that will get you a crown. Just like a fixed mindset, with a poverty mindset, one settles for just enough because you fear that you will never have enough. As a result, you deal with the cards you've been dealt, and you live life in survival mode or from paycheck to paycheck. The poverty mindset becomes a norm, and you learn to cope with any disfunction around your finances. You begin and often complain that you are never and will never have enough.

If I told you Person A makes $60k per year, and Person B makes $160k per year, and asked who was the richest, at first thought most would say Person B. If I asked who was the wealthiest, again most would repeat Person B. The reality is, if Person A is living below their means, putting money into savings and retirement, it's a possibility that they are wealthier than Person B. Why? Suppose Person B doesn't manage their money, invest, nor contribute to savings and retirement, but instead buy luxury items such as cars that'll depreciate. In that case, they'll eventually lose perspective on what they can afford, ultimately living paycheck to paycheck.

The difference is found in the meaning of being wealthy vs. being rich. Rich people spend a lot of money with nothing to show besides what's visible; wealthy people save and invest their money, and most time isn't visible. Quite a few millionaires have gone broke because of their lifestyle; meanwhile, you're over here complaining about wanting a new vehicle while holding the title to what you're currently driving. Perspective is everything, and being strategic is the key to shifting the poverty mentality.

Having a poverty mindset as a Christian is dangerous. You've put limits on God and anything He can do for you. You ignore the possibility that better days are ahead; thus, not allowing yourself to accept those better days because you're covered in despair and living in fear. Perhaps knowing where you come from and the fear of returning to that state physically and financially. Goals, aspirations, and dreams are tossed out the window because anything signifying change or relief becomes hard to attain.

Critical characteristics of someone living with a poverty mindset include but are limited to 1) Having a strong grudge towards those you think are "rich," although you long to be like them, 2) Often complaining about never having enough and how you will never have enough, 3)Thinking small rather than big; immediately placing limitations on what you can or cannot do, 4) Constantly worrying about money and think about it often, 5) Being a cheapskate and depriving yourself of the nice to haves of life, and 6) Always looking for the next quick scheme that may change the situation.

It's amazing how you find clarity when you're on the outside looking in. A conversation around the fear of not having enough or the confidence in abundance, seen in the subtle actions masked behind the colloquial term "I'm on a budget." A group of friends decides to grab lunch and enjoy the comfort of peace and sunshine. Friend A elects to pass on a $6 drink because they're "on a budget," while friend B chooses to purchase a $12 drink, also while being on a budget. The difference here is the mindset of Friend A; a $6 drink cost too much because survival and scarcity is always a lingering thought. Friend A can't see past the fear of poverty or thinking small. The poverty mindset of Friend A will continue to keep them spiraling as they have the mentality that EVERYTHING is too expensive. Nothing is worth it unless it's given free or at a discount.

Meanwhile, Friend B understands the importance of budgeting but doesn't use their budget to deprive themselves of fulfillment and happiness. Friend B fully understands that a budget is a marathon/lifestyle, and with everything comes moderation. In the same way, you should realize that it's okay to treat yourself even if you're on a budget. Just because you spend a few extra dollars to enjoy the money you worked so hard to earn doesn't prohibit you from obtaining the goals you initially set out to accomplish. Lastly, when you are a child of the King, He gets the honor of blessing us, not withholding abundance from us if we walk in/with Him (Psalms 84:11 MSG).

With a poverty mindset, the true definition of winning is never an option because you've already placed limitations on yourself and God. I get it; as someone who grew up in a small town like I, it's common to feel like what you see is normal. If you've never been further than an hour or two from your residence, you are unable to comprehend the endless opportunities waiting on you outside of your comfort zone. Remember where your mind leads you, so will you go. As you begin to renew your mind through the help of the Holy Spirit, you must switch from poverty to a wealthy mindset. To renew your mind, follow these five simple steps:

Decide: Decide today that you want to focus and become better at managing your finances. Your decision should include surrendering your why for God's will.

Control Your Thinking: Expect miracles and expect great things to happen. Become comfortable in God's favor as you begin changing your lifestyle for the better. Spend time with God alone and hide the word of God in your heart (Psalms 119:11). Love, think, and do what is right (Philippians 4:8). Ask the Holy Spirit to lead your thoughts into truth and wisdom.

Control What You're Feeding Your Thoughts: You may have to limit your interaction with certain people, family, and friends. Fill your mind with God's promises and start speaking financial affirmations over yourself daily. Reading God's word and daily devotion with Him will help to ensure that you're digesting and aligning yourself with thoughts of purpose.

Give Yourself Time: Like any mishaps in your financial journey, changes in your mindset will not happen overnight. Don't give up after one incident of failure or setback.

Journal: Begin to commune with God, and during devotion, write down what God says and has promised you. Write down any visions you may see and constantly remind yourself of what God has spoken and shown you. Journaling and writing down what God says will bring you closer to God, and you will give you a clearer view of his will for your life.

The Promise Keeper

In scripture, you can find many promises from God to his people. As Christians, daily, we should be affirming ourselves in the promises of God. His promises are our shield and buckler (Psalms 91:4), meaning we have the tools to combat the enemy when he's trying to speak that which is opposite of God's word. A promise is a declaration that one will perform and do what they've said.

Logan, our 5-year-old son, enjoys going to Target. My husband usually takes him as he is as patient as a fish. He is also great at informing Logan of his budget and will happily tell him if something is out of his budget or if he must exchange something to stay within budget. But whenever Logan asks Daddy if he can go to Target, most likely, my husband will say, "we will go on Friday or Saturday, but we will see." Immediately, you know what Logan's follow-up response is, "You Promise?". That is his way of confirming that what daddy has told him is true. We all know that we can't make a promise to a child and not follow through because they will hold us to it.

Therefore, God said we should come to Him as children. God has made multiple promises to us, his children, and knowing that He's not a man that can lie, our only job is to believe and receive. In the Bible, you can find one of the most significant promises in Matthew 6:33, "But seek ye first the kingdom of God and his righteousness, and all these things will be added to you." This scripture makes me happy knowing that seeking the kingdom of God and his righteousness opens the door to all my requirements and needs, including my financial needs. God promised us in Philippians 4:19 that He would supply all our needs according to his riches in glory in Christ Jesus. Applying God's promises can lead you out of debt and towards financial freedom. Let's dissect a few more scriptures and what our responsibility is to receive the promise:

Proverbs 3:9-10 (NLT)
Command: Honor the Lord with your wealth and with the best part of everything you produce.
Promise: He will fill your barns with grain, and your vats will overflow with good wine.

Deuteronomy 8:18 (NLT)
Command: Remember the Lord Your God
Promise: He is the one who gives you the power to be successful; to fulfill the covenant, He confirmed to your ancestors with an oath.

2 Corinthians 9:6-12 (NLT)
Command: Plan generously; you must decide in your heart how much to give. Don't give reluctantly or in response to

pressure. For God loves a person who gives cheerfully.
Promise: Reap generous crop; God will generously provide all you need. Then you will always have everything you need and plenty left over to share with others.

Proverbs 3:6 (NLT)
Command: Seek his will in all you do
Promise: He will show you which path to take.

Luke 6:38 (NLT)
Command: Give
Promise: You will receive; your gift will return to you in full – pressed down, shaken together to make room for more, running over, and poured into your lap. The amount you give will determine the amount you get back.

Malachi 3:10-12 (NLT)
Command: Bring all the tithes into the storehouse so there will be enough food in our Temple.
Promise: If you do, says the Lord of Heaven's Armies, I will open the windows of heaven for you. I will pour out a blessing so great that you won't have enough room to take it in! Try it! Put me to the test. Your crops will be abundant, for I will guard them against insects and disease. Your grapes will not fall from the vine before they are ripe. Then all nations will call you blessed, for your land will be such a delight, says the Lord of Heaven's Armies.

Matthew 6:33 (NLT)
Command: Seek the Kingdom of God above all else, and live righteously,
Promise: He will give you everything you need.

I Am Rich; I Am Wealthy

Please repeat after me; I AM WEALTHY!!! Now say it with some authority. To fully understand the magnitude of natural wealth, you must know that you're wealthy spiritually. To be wealthy in Christ should be our greatest desire. We fail to understand Christ's love for us and the wealth and riches we possess in Him. As my pastor preached this message, "Membership Has Its Privileges," he reminded us that in Ephesians, we find that while also being showered and soaked with God's kindness, Christ has chosen us for greatness. He tells us that we've been marked with the Holy Spirit and filled with the power of the Holy Spirit.

We are God's masterpiece and included in God's grand plan. Ephesians 1:3-6 (MSG) says, "How blessed is God! And what a blessing He is! He's the Father of our Master, Jesus Christ, and takes us to the high places of blessing in Him. Long before He laid down earth's foundations, He had us in mind, had settled on us as the focus of his love, to be made whole and holy by his love. Long, long ago, He decided to adopt us into his family through Jesus Christ. (What pleasure He took in planning this!) He wanted us to enter into the celebration of his lavish gift-giving by the hand of his beloved Son."

No matter what someone else may have, I understand that I am wealthy, and I don't have to play second to anyone. We find in 2 Corinthians 8:9 that when Jesus became mankind, He became poor for us to be rich and wealthy and to experience the wealth, riches, and security of God. God has blessed us immensely, so much that we can't count the blessings He has in store for us.

As you go throughout the day, tell yourself that you're wealthy. Wealthy in Christ while also being wealthy in all aspects of your life, even your finances. As we've already stated, God owns EVERYTHING. I really want that to sink in. God is complete, and through Him, we are also complete. No matter who He gives riches to, it doesn't change how much He has or doesn't deplete his worth. Think about it, we've heard of millionaires and billionaires, but have you ever heard of anyone being called a trillionaire, quadrillionaire, quintillionaire? Yet God is worth more than googolplex; his worth is infinite, meaning his worth can't be assigned a number. So, the meaning of everything goes beyond what we can even imagine.

For most people who had wealthy parents who looked out for their well-being, their children reaped the benefits of their wealth. They were taken good care of, had a good number of their wants, food on their table, and a trust set aside for them to enjoy life just as their parents had, most times even better. How much greater do you think our heavenly Father has already done for us if these are earthly parents.

When God sent his only begotten Son to die for our sins, we were all immediately given access to our trust. We didn't have to wait until we were a certain age or status. While we were yet sinners, Christ died for us (Romans 5:8). Just as a parent would expect their child or children to manage their trust account responsibly, God expects us to do the same. Understand and use the resources He's made available responsibly.

When you receive a trust or inheritance, you have every single advantage favoring your direction. You can essentially do and have anything you like knowing you're secure. When you don't have, ask; what you can't find, seek. Allow the peace of God and all that He's given you access to to fill your hearts and spirits.

Spiritually you are rich in God's grace and mercy, and you have an inheritance. We are enjoying the compliments of God's grace and the blood Christ shed. So as your days are, so will your strength be! Don't let the world fool you into thinking that because you don't have what they have, you're operating in lack. Once we fully understand how rich we are in Christ, we can then put into perspective and fully understand earthly riches. Understanding the prioritization and that you're rich spiritually, the earthly riches will follow.

CHAPTER 4: STRATEGIC STEWARDSHIP

As each has received a gift, use it to serve one another, as good
stewards of God's varied grace:

-1 PETER 4:10 (ESV)

One of our responsibilities as Christians is to be great stewards over the things God has given us through blessings. Stewardship means honoring God with our possessions and managing them his way. I remember my mom often said, "God will not bless you with new if you can't take care of what you have." That has stuck with me, and even when the kids get my car a little, okay maybe a lot junky, because kids don't have any chill, I think, Lord let me get this car clean; I never know when my new car is coming. I laugh about it at times, but it's the ultimate gesture of appreciation for what you have.

If you gave someone a lovely gift and they were mistreating it or damaging it, you would certainly have to pray about giving that person anything else. Our job is to ensure that we are great stewards of our lives, belongings, and especially our children. As someone who experienced a miscarriage, I promised God that when I did get pregnant, I would do all I could to make sure that I was appreciative of Him blessing us with a child. What better way to show God that you're thankful for his blessings than to show appreciation?

But the first thing is to realize that God owns EVERYTHING (have you heard this before), and as a result, everything that we have comes from Him. He has equipped us with management skills and made us managers, so think of yourself as head manager instead of the owner. A manager is responsible for taking care of and overseeing something on someone else's behalf. You have free will and authority that aligns with the purpose of creation, but you still work for the owner (Luke 12:42-43).

As parents, when someone gives your child a gift or piece of candy, we immediately say, "Did you say Thank You?" We'll ask the person giving the present, "Did they tell you Thank You?" and if our children don't say it loud enough, we sometimes take it out of their hands and make them redo it all over again. God should never have to snatch anything from us because we fail to say thank you. We find this in the story of The Great Flood in Genesis 6-9. We fail to experience the true blessings of God because we try to take ownership over our lives; we put our "why" ahead of his will.

The Parable of the Talents found in Matthew 25:14-30 is an excellent example of stewardship and management. In this very familiar passage, the master leaves his servants in charge while he's on a journey, leaving one with five talents, another with two talents, and the last with one talent. Once the master returns, he assesses each servant and how they've managed what was left for them. He rewards them based on how faithful and wise each one is with their talents.

Two out of the three servants put their talents to work and doubled the value. In verse 23, the servant says, "Well done, good and faithful servant; thou hast been faithful over a few things; I will make thee ruler over many things: enter thou into the joy of thy lord." The third servant, given one talent, decided to bury his talent and hide it in the ground. Verse 26 and 27, we find that the master was furious. He stated, "That's a terrible way to live! It's criminal to live cautiously like that! If you knew I was after the best, why did you do less than the least? The least you could have done would have been to invest the sum with the bankers, where at least I would have gotten a little interest." It sounds like the last servant had a poverty and scarcity mindset.

What the servants had was not their own, and their only job was to manage what the master had left them. We must be cautious not to misuse or abuse what God has given us based on our thoughts but remember that everything we have belongs to God and must be treated as such. This parable does a great job of showing us that it doesn't matter about the quantity. We often look at our neighbors and, because they have more, assume stewardship is only for the one with greater.

No matter how much or little you have, it's still your responsibility to manage it. Being a great steward has nothing to do with how well you're able to do something; if you're unable to use it or show it, what's the purpose of having the gift?

There is a reward for honoring God with all He has given us. When we die, we will be judged on the possessions we receive on earth and throughout our life. Like the servants, we will be judged on how wisely we used our talents, time, and money granted to us. Stewardship isn't always easy, but it's worth it. Come here, Noah; we want to ask you how easy it was to build the ark.

When commanded to build the ark, take one of each kind of animal, and protect his family from the flood, he did just that. He managed the building of God's ark through criticism and all assigned to him while on the ark. Noah could've easily done what he wanted to do, handled the animals how he thought they should've been dealt, or even told God, "You know I don't do the felines, so I am just going to leave them off." However, Noah understood the assignment, his role as manager, and God as the owner; thus, he was saved and received all the blessings of being a great steward.

I don't know about you, but for me, there is an overwhelming feeling of confidence and joy knowing I'm doing the right thing, especially knowing that God sees all and is the ultimate rewarder of all. Nothing we have, have we contributed, merited, or done to deserve it. Doing right feels good if you ask me. Are you being a good steward and using your talents to double their worth? Or like the one servant, burying or mismanaging your talent?

The link between stewardship and managing your finances

Being a great steward of your finances means managing your finances in God's way. God wants us to work and be willing to take risks for his name's sake; He wants us to continue building, increasing, and multiplying what He has given us. Your blessings are connected to your actions, and stewardship is an action word. God has given us the responsibility of managing our finances and household. He doesn't want us neglecting our mortgage or rent to go on vacation; or refusing to pay the debt we owe because we feel the need to use the funds elsewhere. As Christians, not only do we have to be great stewards, but strategic stewards. Strategic means being diligent and carefully planning for a particular purpose. When you're strategic, you make decisions based on evidence and what you know to be true.

As Christians, what do we know to be true? We know that God owns everything (there it goes again); we know that God has promised us the ability to produce wealth and order our steps; we know that God will never leave us, and we know that we have a responsibility of being great stewards. So, what's holding you back from agreeing now to decide and surrender to God's will for your life? Repent now for the ways you've used your money that was ungodly. Repent for neglecting to be responsible stewards over what God has given you. Repent for not appreciating and expressing to God your thankfulness for what He's provided. Lastly, repent for the times you ignored leading of the Holy Spirit and didn't give or bless someone when instructed to do so.

Finances are one of the most significant responsibilities and areas of stewardship. Often, we want more but can't be trusted with $1,000, let alone $10,000. We pray for a breakthrough and will often say, "I could do so much better if I just had more" when you're poorly managing what you have. While there is some truth in that statement, I'm sure we could all accept more; but where is your mindset? Have you written down all your debt and are paying towards it? For example, if you're in debt and offered $10,000, would you be able to confidently pinpoint an amount to put towards debt and know precisely which category or item of debt? We will learn later that some debt is unavoidable; however, it's not about the amount but about how you manage it and your plan to get out of debt.

Being a great steward has a lot to do with changing your mindset, committing to being your best self, confidence, and trust. You have to talk to God and be honest with Him by saying, "God, I am managing my money responsibly and as you've instructed me to do so. I trust that you will supply all of my needs, and I will not experience lack." Does anyone else talk to God like this? He knows our true hearts anyway, and for me, talking to God as if we commune every day (because we do) and He's sitting beside me (because He is) makes our conversations natural and easier. Think about it: is it possible that you do not have because God can't trust you to manage it well, according to how He has directed you? Don't forget; you're the manager, not the owner; know your role.

There are principles and promises to being a good steward over our finances.

- **Managing**– Diligently planning leads to profit; haste leads to poverty – Proverbs 21:5
- **Saving**– A wise man saves for the future–Proverbs 21:20
- **Giving**– A generous man will be blessed–Proverbs 22:9
- **Trusting**– Trusting God leads to prosperity–Proverbs 30:8-9
- **Working**– All hard work leads to profit–Proverbs 14:23
- **Providing**– Provide for your household – 1 Timothy 5:8
- **Receiving**– It's good to receive wealth from God – Ecclesiastes 5:19

CHAPTER 5: OUR RESPONSIBILITY TO GOD

Honor the Lord with your wealth and with the firstfruits of all your produce;

PROVERBS 3:9 (ESV)

It's testimony time. After my husband proposed, I immediately prayed to God and said, Lord, you'll have to help us pay for this wedding. As you read in the first chapter, putting the responsibility of the wedding of my dreams on my parents wasn't even an option. My husband proposed a little over a year after graduating from college, and I was working my dream job as an IT Analyst. My income probably tripled that of my parents, so sticking to the tradition of the bride's parents paying for the wedding didn't faze me.

As I began looking at venues, of course, I looked at the best and most expensive venue first. Why did I do this? As a Certified Wedding Planner and a little suggestion for my brides, this is not good practice. And as you would expect, each venue I visited afterward never compared to THE one. After sitting down with my now-husband, he understood what I wanted and understood that 1) we would be paying for the wedding and 2) using credit wasn't an option.

As a couple, we decided that we would put $1,000 in savings a month, and that would be enough over the next year or so to pay for wedding expenses. And of course, just knowing the bit about my parents from reading, they were not going to let me have an entire wedding without them contributing. You might ask, "What does this have to do with our responsibility to God?" At the start of setting aside money for our wedding, we also decided to give more to God in tithes and offerings. Now that I think back, I'm still surprised at the fact that we really did that! Additionally, my husband and I decided we would pay off our gross instead of our net pay during that time.

When I say God overflowed in our lives in more ways than one, the testimonies we have and the blessings we received are beyond what we could imagine. For one, although not asked, my parents paid for my wedding dress and contributed money here and there based on what they could afford. Secondly, we were able to have the wedding at THE venue, and most importantly, we incurred no debt due to us getting married; that isn't everyone's testimony.

Lastly, we were getting married in March, and the November before, we decided to buy a single-family home instead of renting an apartment which was our original plan. We made this decision the week before Thanksgiving. Some say God looks out for babies and fools, and I think we fit into both of those categories as a young couple getting married in a little over three months. We began looking at houses with our realtor and finally came across a home that we loved; unfortunately, it was a short sale. A short sale is when the buyer sells the house for less than the remaining balance on the mortgage.

The most important thing here is that back in the day; it was 2012; short sales took up to six months to make it to the closing table because of all the paperwork and reviews that had to be done by the seller's lender. However, we felt the push from God to move forward. We put in the offer a week before Christmas, understanding that it was the holiday season and that most bankers would be out of the office the last two weeks of the year. When completing our paperwork, our mortgage officer also put TBD for the closing date, knowing that it would take a minimum of three months even to hear back and move forward. On January 18th, I remember it like it was yesterday. This is the same day my niece was born; we received notification that the seller's lender accepted our offer. There were a few adjustments as they informed us they weren't able to pay the $4,975 we'd requested for closing, but let's say God worked it out. Our loan officer immediately called us and said, "My God, someone must be living right; I've never seen a short sale processed this quick."

Additionally, what shocked him even more, we only put down $1,000 in earnest money, and for some reason (God), we were due $566.24 at closing. I had to go look that number up as I made sure to keep the paperwork and emails for when I unconsciously think about putting brakes on what God can do. We closed on February 9th, 2012, got married on March 3rd, 2012, and were able to move into our relatively new 4-bedroom home, three years old to be exact, for only $433.76. And not that we deserved anything else; that house is currently one of our investment properties. Looking at the goodness of God, we didn't know at the time why God was telling us to give Him more while trying to pay for a wedding and start life as a married couple, but now we see. Also, I believe God honored us for not forcing or being mad that my parents didn't pay for our wedding, although as stated, they still contributed. I now understand the statement that says you can't beat God's giving, no matter how hard you try.

Tithing

Because we serve a generous God, our money is also one of many ways to show our generosity to Him; most of the time, a way that is hard for most. Sadly, many have confused tithing and offering with giving to the Pastor, not to God. The church's reputation has been dramatically destroyed due to the idolization of money, which has ultimately become a breeding ground for greed. Unfortunately, some holding this sacred title will say whatever they can to make parishioners give; again, all for the wrong reasons. Giving tithes and offering is a principle that has been around for a long time and frankly will continue to stick around.

There are still many questions around whether Christians should tithe, how much one should tithe, the difference between tithe and offering, Old Testament vs. New Testament, and the list continues. Let's start with tithing. Tithing has been defined as giving ten percent of your first fruit, or in basic terms, to give ten percent of your income, earnings, or possessions to your church or ministry. Some people argue that tithing is less or more than ten percent; however, if we want to be literal, tithing is Hebrew for the tenth, but please do not get stuck on the tenth concept. The reality is, we can never out-give God.

We first come across the principle of tithing in Genesis 14 starting at verse 18; later recapped in Hebrews 7. As Abraham returns from battle with everything he has retrieved from war, he's greeted by Melchizedek, king of Salem, with bread, wine, and blessings. Here is where Abraham presents Melchizedek with a tenth of all the treasures he has retrieved, ultimately showing his appreciation to God for his grace, helping him, and pronouncing blessings over his life. Melchizedek is one mentioned in the Bible who many religious scholars find mysterious and exciting because he suddenly appears on the scene as King and Priest of God Most High. Known as the King of Salem, meaning king of righteousness; without father or mother, descent, having neither beginning of days, nor end of life; but made like unto the Son of God (Hebrews 7:1-3). Some believed the first appearance of God himself, taking the form of man and said to be similar to the Son of God.

So one may say that Abraham wasn't just paying his tenth to an ordinary king or person. Additional scriptures where we find tithing mentioned in the Bible is Leviticus 27:30 (MSG), "a tenth of the land's produce, whether grain from the ground or fruit from the trees, is God's" and Proverbs 3:9-10 (MSG) "honor God with everything you own; give Him the first and the best. Your barns will burst, your wine vats will brim over." When mentioned that your tithe should be your first fruit, one is essentially saying to God, thank you for all your blessings. I'm setting this amount aside first, ahead of any bills, expenses, needs, or wants, understanding that it is through your love and grace that I'm able to attain and acquire wealth.

Your tithes should be set aside before budgeting, putting money towards debt, or even giving to others. Thus, giving and managing our finances is one of the most significant areas of stewardship. Tithing is your form of worship to God. We often sing, "I Love You, Jesus, I worship and adore you, just want to tell you that I love you more than anything." That, more than anything, includes our money and finances. Ultimately, we're saying we trust Him (not our money) to provide everything we need. We aren't just giving God money when we tithe because technically, He already owns it. We're simply honoring and giving God back a portion of what He has given us.

Offering

On the other hand, an offering is anything extra or that which is given beyond your tithes in or outside of the church. This is another form of expressing generosity throughout the body of Christ. Your offering is designated for the community, ministries within the church, or mission depending on the ministry. Most would like to think that tithing is a specific amount that God has instructed us to give while the offering is given at our free will and based on our ability to give (after our first fruit). This would be equivalent to planting just a few more seeds to attain a larger harvest. You may think of paying tithes only after receiving income and offering each time you attend Sunday worship, an act of generosity or giving to support a mission.

As tithing is specified in the Bible as a tenth, the amount required for offering has never been specified. There isn't a commandment in the Bible to give offering; it just commands us to be generous and cheerful in our giving. 2 Corinthians 9:7 (NLT) says, "You must each decide in your heart how much to give; not giving reluctantly or in response to pressure. "For God loves a person who gives cheerfully." Tithes and offerings are different regarding the specificity of the frequency and amount; however, both determine your heart posture and trust towards God.

The Bible repeatedly tells us that our giving is an extension of our faith, keyword, extension. Meaning it doesn't take the place of our relationship with God. We shouldn't be as The Pharisee found in the parable of The Pharisee and Tax

Collector in Luke 18:9-14. Tax collectors were despised, especially by the Pharisees, and were regarded as sinners because they were Jews who cheated people out of their money, all while working for the Romans. In this parable, Jesus talks about two men, a Pharisee, and a tax collector, who entered the temple to pray. The Pharisee, of course, being one who cared more about tradition, prayed about himself, how he'd done everything according to the book, including paying his tenth and how he was nothing like the tax collector. However, the tax collector humbled himself and prayed for God's grace while admitting he was a sinner.

No matter how much we fast, attend church, stick to tradition, or pay our tithes and offering, no amount of good works can replace a simple posture of surrendering to God. Jesus shows us that although despised by many, the tax collector returned as a righteous man because he humbled himself before Him. What purpose would it be for us to gain the world and lose our souls? (Matthew 16:26). To faithfully fast and give to the church, but on judgment day, God says, "depart from me, I never knew you"? Giving to God is our way of acknowledging that we trust Him with every facet of our lives, including our finances. Lastly, it is excellent for us to give back to God through our giving, but there is also a responsibility from the church to its members, community, and most importantly, God to accomplish what God has called the church to do.

Is It Still Required? Old Vs. New Testament

As you may recall, according to VancoFaith, only 1.5 million people out of the 247 million people identified as Christians pay their tithes. Ironically, most Christians do not pay tithes. Many Christians would argue that paying tithes is under the old law that Christians are no longer required to practice. Tithing is more spiritual than financial as God loves a cheerful giver. He would rather for you not to give than to give grudgingly. I don't think one should decide whether giving is biblically based on the suggestion of old vs. new law.

In Luke 11:42, Jesus informs us that it's a matter of the heart. Yes, tithing should be a routine if we're giving from the heart out of appreciation for the grace God has given us, and not just an afterthought when you see you have money left over. However, you're hopeless and a fraud if you're careless about fairness, compassion, and commitment, the basics to serving God.

Once you determine that tithing is a posture of your heart, you aren't focused on whether it's the old or new law, or ten percent, but paying according to what God has instructed you to give. Jesus teaches us in Mark 12:41-44 about the widow giving her last. In this scripture, Jesus is sitting across from the offering box and observing the crowd and their giving. He observed the rich giving significant contributions, but a poor widow immediately caught his attention. Although she only gave two small coins, Jesus called his disciples over and explained to them that the poor widow, although the least in amount, gave more to the collection than all the rich people combined.

He continues to elaborate and explain that the rich people gave what they didn't need or will never miss; however, the widow extravagantly gave what she couldn't afford; she gave her all. In this passage, Jesus teaches us not to get caught up in the specifics or the amount according to law but rather the sacrifices made when given. Lift your hands and ask God to help you be like the poor widow, to give all you have in ALL areas of your life.

The great thing about giving to God is that man can never tell you what's too little or too much. For one, only God knows the posture of your heart, and God can see what man overlooks. In the widow's case, God was able to see yet small the abundance and humbleness of her gift. Secondly, God doesn't add nor calculate like humankind. In this passage of scripture, although the widow gave two coins or two cents, in the eyes of God, it was more than the total given by all the rich givers. How amazing is this? When you think that what you have isn't enough, God tells you that it's more than enough. More than your neighbor who may be driving the nice car and living in the nice house, while you may be thinking about the source of your next meal.

This parable should compel us as givers to constantly stay in prayer and devotion with God to hear His will for our lives and giving. Ask God for wisdom in your giving. The flip side to that is God knows when we're obedient and when we're not. Being a cheerful giver and following God's lead is the ultimate example of true devotion. God is faithful to do just what He said He would do. If you want to experience the promises of God you read about, stop focusing on the law; follow the leading of God's voice in your life.

Sowing & Reaping

In the natural land, to sow is to plant crops, while reaping is gathering those crops: the more seed planted, the more crop available during harvest. Simply put, you get more when you give or put down more! 2 Corinthians 9:6-7 (MSG) says, "Remember: A stingy planter gets a stingy crop; a lavish planter gets a lavish crop. Please take plenty of time to think it over and make up your mind about what you will give. That will protect you against sob stories and arm-twisting. God loves it when the giver delights in the giving." Verses 10-11 encourage us that He who supplies seed to the sower and bread for food will also supply and increase your store of seed and enlarge the harvest of your righteousness. You will be enriched in every way so that you can be generous on every occasion, and through us, your generosity will result in thanksgiving to God. When thinking about our harvest, this also includes joy, happiness, along with our physical needs/wants.

Jesus speaks in Matthew 13:8 about your harvest being multiplied by a hundred, sixty, or thirty times what was sowed. Giving to someone should internally make you happy and encourage you to continue your acts of giving in the long run. Think about it; maybe we don't have more of what we desire because we refuse to give God what He wants. There is an old saying that says, "a closed mouth doesn't get fed." Essentially, you can't expect to receive if your hands are closed, and you're not willing and open to reciprocating the action.

Luke 6:38 tells us, "Give, and you will receive. Your gift will return to you in full, pressed down, shaken together to make room for more, running over, and poured into your lap. The amount you give will determine the amount you get back." Knowing that God isn't a man who lies, neither is He the son of man who must repent, I stand on his promises and will decide to be obedient to his word. There has always been a notion that money and spirituality don't exist together.

Understanding the spiritual side of our finances, our responsibility to God, his promises, principles, and commands allows us to manage our earthly possessions better. There must be a balance mentally for one not to supersede the other. You never want your money to come before your spirituality; however, you never want to over-spiritualize lack in your life and choose to ignore your lack of financial obedience. Jesus puts it simple in Acts 20:35 by saying, "It is more blessed to give than to receive." Some blessings will only come from your participation in the process. What kind of seeds are you sowing? Being generous is an excellent sign that your money doesn't control you.

CHAPTER 6: THE BORROWER VS. THE LENDER

For God so loved the world, that he gave his only Son, that whoever believes in him should not perish but have eternal life.

JOHN 3:16 (NIV)

The Borrower

Let's be honest with ourselves here! Everyone isn't fortunate enough to be able to purchase a home with cash. Let us be clear; some people can do this at the snap of a finger, but unfortunately, that isn't mine nor half of America's testimony. Does that mean we shouldn't borrow money or work to ensure we have a roof over our heads? Does this mean you shouldn't desire a lovely home? Absolutely not. Because of this, when we are required to borrow money—due to situations in our lives such as medical emergencies, how we grew up, and our current conditions such as a job layoff, becoming a borrower is sometimes unavoidable.

Nevertheless, we should always be striving or working to become debt-free. The reality is that reducing your debt increases your financial security. When you pay off your debt, you have more money to save or pay other expenses more easily should you experience an unexpected drop in your income. As my grandma would say, "You need not owe any man but God." Many read the scripture Romans 13:8 (KJV), which states, "Owe no man anything, but to love one another: for he that loveth another hath fulfilled the law." Unfortunately, it becomes confusing, and many raise an eyebrow assuming that God prohibits financial debt or taking on debt. I like the way the NIV version of the scripture interprets the text, "Let no debt remain outstanding, except the continuing debt to love one another, for whoever loves others has fulfilled the law." The keyword here is outstanding!

The Bible makes it clear that when you borrow, it becomes a master and servant relationship. If the debt is outstanding, you as the borrower/servant owe, and the lender/master controls the outcome of a specific piece of your future if you decide not to pay. For example, when you purchase a home, the bank will take your home and possibly everything in it if you choose not to pay your mortgage. It will go on your record as a foreclosure, possibly affecting your ability to purchase another home in the future. The same with loan or credit card debt; at the end of the day, if you do not pay, sending it over to the Credit Bureau is only the tap of a key, thus affecting your ability to obtain goods on credit in the future. In these cases, you are a servant to the debtor until it's fully paid.

Secondly, the Bible teaches us to solidify a repayment plan when we borrow money. Psalms 37:21 tells us that the wicked borrows but does not pay back, but the righteous is generous and gives. In this scripture, we see that it isn't the act of borrowing that's wicked; it's the one that doesn't pay back after borrowing that's wicked. Meaning before taking on new debt, we should ensure the means to repay are available. Some of us have been guilty of saying, "they'll get their money when they get it," and this is the wrong attitude to have, no matter if it's a corporation, friend, or family member. When you sign the papers and commit to making those monthly payments by a set date, you have a responsibility to God and to the lender to make that payment.

Just like paying tithes and managing your finances, borrowing money is another act of stewardship. The justification of borrowing is based on the concept of our hearts, if we're borrowing wisely or not. Thus, the reason why before taking on new debt, there are ten questions you should always ponder and review before making a decision:

1. What is the purpose of this purchase? Why do I need it? What will happen if I do not borrow this money to achieve this purchase?

2. Have I prayed about this to ensure it aligns with God's will for my life?

3. Have I chosen the most cost-effective option for borrowing? Have I shopped around to determine what is best for me?

4. Will this item I'm purchasing last as long as it will take me to repay? If it takes me ten years to make the payment, can I expect it to last longer than ten years, or will I have to start looking for something else?

5. Will this purchase appreciate (i.e., home) or depreciate (i.e., car) in value?

6. What will my monthly payment be, and can I afford it?

7. Have I thought about additional requirements not included in the monthly payment (i.e., insurance, utilities, other interest, etc.)?

8. What is my interest rate, and how much interest will I pay over the life of the loan?

9. What bucket is the money required for payment coming from (emergency fund, retirement, extra cash on hand, etc.), and what is my payoff plan?

10. Do I need it right now (delayed gratification)? Can I perhaps wait to save more to lower my monthly payment? Are there any reasons that require me to get it right now?

11. Will borrowing from a friend or family member strain our relationship? Am I taking advantage of their generosity?

The Bible also warns against surety or making yourself responsible for the debt belonging to someone else. Surety would be equivalent to being a cosigner or becoming a guarantor on a loan in today's terms. Proverbs 17:18 says one who has no sense shakes hands in pledge and puts up security for a neighbor. There are, unfortunately, possible financial and emotional implications in surety. The reality is you can't become financially secure by being the financial security for your neighbor.

Ultimately, although the Bible doesn't state that borrowing money is a sin, it does warn us about the implications of borrowing. Therefore, we should always ensure that our intentions are pure and in line with God's will for our lives. He tells us in Philippians 4:19 that He will supply all of our needs according to his riches in glory by Christ Jesus. If you do not have to borrow, don't. If you must borrow, make sure you have a well-considered repayment plan in place that aligns with what you're able to afford. Lastly, as God our savior and provider, we should always seek God for provision.

Ways to Pay off Debt

As mentioned, we should always be looking for ways to become debt-free, as that is the will of God. What are some proven methods to help you pay off debt?

- Identify and list your debt. Make a list of your debts, including interest rates and the amount and frequency of payments for each one.

- Budget. Ensure that you've budgeted enough funds to cover your minimum payments so that you avoid late fees, additional charges, and damage to your credit rating. Once you create and establish a budget and set goals, paying off debt becomes manageable.

- Decide on a debt payment strategy that works for you. There are a few well-known strategies but deciding which works best for you is key.

  - **Debt Snowball:** Focuses on debt with the smallest balance. Continue making minimum payments and putting extra money towards the smallest balance. Once you've paid off the smallest debt/balance and the money is free, roll that money into the NEXT SMALLEST DEBT and continue to repeat until you are debt-free. With this option, you'll see progress quickly.

  - **Debt Avalanche:** Focuses on debt with the highest interest rate. Continue making minimum payments and putting extra money toward the balance with the highest interest rate. Once you've paid off the debt/ balance with the highest interest rate and the money is free, roll that money to the NEXT HIGHEST INTEREST RATE DEBT. With this option, you'll pay less interest.

NOTE: IF YOU HAVE TROUBLE STAYING MOTIVATED TO PAY OFF DEBT, DEBT SNOWBALL IS BETTER FOR YOU.

- If you can't find money in your current budget to pay off your debt, look for ways to increase your income rather than raiding your retirement accounts.

The most important thing to remember is that once you are out of debt, plan to use that money to help you achieve your financial goals. Rather than splurging on unnecessary expenses, or going back into debt, take the money you no longer need to spend on debt repayment and use it to increase your savings or purchase long-term assets that increase your wealth. When you increase your income, as long as you keep your expenses the same or reduce them, you'll have more money to achieve most financial goals.

The Lender

You're sitting at home, enjoying your morning coffee and devotion, and your phone rings. You look down and in distaste because you know exactly why this person is calling. Most likely, they've hit yet another bump in the road and need to borrow a few dollars until Friday. This type of call may sound familiar. It doesn't feel great at times; however, the silver lining is that we should rather be on the side of lending instead of borrowing. In Church, we often repeat God's word found in Deuteronomy 28:12 and state that God shall make us a lender and not a borrower.

Before we dig deeper, being a lender isn't to be confused with abuse, misuse, or an enabler. God should always be our provider and the source of our needs. Even in between the stages of progressing, working, and changing life for my family and me, I had to quickly realize that I couldn't play God and couldn't always be superwoman. In particular, while trying to be the resource, I became the source. When I stepped in while God was trying to teach a lesson, I quickly realized that we both were at a loss, but I digressed.

The Bible clarifies, and as we have learned, borrowing money opens the line to that of a servant relationship. The most significant moral we should learn from lending in the Bible is to help out the poor and needy. For example, someone losing their job and income is supporting the needy. When we do this, we lend, not looking for anything in return, knowing that God will be the source of our repayment and with unlimited interest.

The problem is when we lend to our friends and family who mismanaged their money because they decided to take a vacation instead of paying their bills or needed the latest item and are now in need of assistance. We are discouraged from lending money to anyone in these situations, including the poor. Cases like this are where relationships with friends and family are ruined. I read a quote that said, when borrowing money from friends and family, decide at that time, which is more important, the relationship or the money.

Lending was not discouraged. Psalms 112: 5-6 (NIV) says, "Good will come to those who are generous and lend freely, who conduct their affairs with justice. Surely the righteous will never be shaken; they will be remembered forever." This is God's promise to us that as long as we're lending with a pure heart that He will not forget us. Just as a borrower can request with a wicked heart, so can that be the heart of a lender. We have to be careful not to use our position as a lender as a means of control.

Lending With or Without Interest

The next question becomes whether you should lend with or without interest. Let me make this clear; we are talking biblically. As a Christian who works for a financial institution, please do not walk into the bank and tell them that they are sinners and you are not paying interest on your loan. They will most likely tell you that your loan has been denied and to leave their bank. As lenders, we are responsible for following God's words just the same as we do with managing our money. The Bible gives explicit warnings to lending without interest to those who are poor or unable to pay. In Exodus 22:25 (KJV), God tells us that if thou lend money to any of my people that is poor by thee, thou shalt not be to him as a usurer, neither shalt thou lay upon him usury.

Usury is a common word used today, meaning illegal lending at an unreasonable or high-interest rate. It was preventing the lender from gaining an unfair profit from the loan. As found in scripture, usury had a slightly different meaning; this was the lending of interest of any kind. During this time, requiring fellow Jews to pay interest on loans wasn't beneficial for the economy as it could perhaps put them more in debt. The only exception was loaning to foreigners, as interest was allowed. Each religion has different views when it comes to usuary and charging interest.

The goal was to remind the Jews that helping the poor and needy can and should be done without expecting anything in return. Whether or not interest should be charged is determined by our heart posture. Luke 6:34-35 (MSG) sums it up best for us by saying, "here is a simple rule of thumb for behavior: Ask yourself what you want people to do for you; then grab the initiative and do it for them! If you only love the lovable, do you expect a pat on the back? Run-of-the-mill sinners do that. If you only help those who help you, do you expect a medal? Garden-variety sinners do that. If you only give for what you hope to get out of it, do you think that's charity?

The stingiest of pawnbrokers does that. I tell you, love your enemies. Help and give without expecting a return. You'll never—I promise—regret it. Live out this God-created identity the way our Father lives toward us, generously and graciously, even when we're at our worst. Our Father is kind; you be kind."

God showed us the most remarkable example of being a lender when He gave his Son. John 3:16-18 (MSG) tells us that this is how much God loved the world: He gave his Son, his one and only Son. And therefore: so that no one need be destroyed; by believing in Him, anyone can have a whole and lasting life. God didn't go through all the trouble of sending his Son merely to point an accusing finger, telling the world how bad it was. He came to help, to put the world right again. Anyone who trusts in Him is acquitted; anyone who refuses to trust Him has long since been under the death sentence without knowing it. And why? Because of that person's failure to believe in the one-of-a-kind Son of God when introduced to Him. When we begin to think about this 33-year loan that had more impact than any of us can have in our lifetime combined, we understand how lending a few dollars without interest is small compared to that God lent to us. He even left an extra comforter, the Holy Spirit, to lead and guide us.

What is Credit?

Today, interest rates have a strong correlation with your creditworthiness. Your credit score and the use of credit cards are top discussions regarding your finances—another correlation between paying off your debt and being good stewards. Credit is the ultimate temptation for us to spend money we do not have. Managing our money responsibly and God's way has a way of showing up in other areas of our financial journey. If we're obeying God's instructions for handling debt, working towards paying off debt, and making payments on time, we should all be looking at 800 or 850 credit scores. Unfortunately, this isn't the case as, according to Experian, almost half of consumers have a credit score less than 700. To get started, let's explore credit and why it's essential.

Credit is simply the ability of a consumer to obtain goods or services before payment based on the trust that the consumer will make the payment in the future. Credit ultimately determines how good you are at keeping the promise of paying your debt. Your credit score is a number between 300 and 850 and represents your ability to repay your debt. The data on each of your reports are analyzed to assign a credit score. A high credit score confirms that you are a low-risk borrower and most likely to repay. A low credit score suggests that you are a high-risk risk borrower and less likely to repay. As a result, if you have a low credit score, your interest rate is most likely higher. If you have a high credit score, you will find that your interest rate is lower.

We've established that for some of us, buying items on credit is sometimes required. So why is knowing this important,

300 to 579	580 to 669	670 to 739	740 to 799	800 to 850
BAD	POOR	FAIR	GOOD	EXCELLENT

besides ensuring that we're working towards a debt-free life? Your creditworthiness is reviewed by financial institutions, employers, cellular and utility companies, rental properties, and many others. Sometimes it's the difference between having to pay or pay an additional deposit. Creditors make a judgment about your ability to repay and decide whether they want to extend credit to you and at what interest rate. Avoiding negative records like late payments and unpaid balances helps sustain a good credit rapport. Credit isn't bad because you need credit to prove that you're responsible and establish a credit history.

Whether or not you believe carrying debt or buying on credit is a sin, credit scores are becoming an important number in your journey to financial wellness. However, as Christians, we must have more trust in God than in our credit cards. Sometimes we entangle ourselves when we use our credit cards to purchase something God has already told us not to buy (yep, the money isn't there on purpose). Or, sometimes, instead of praying about our next move, we use our credit card, knowing the money is available, accessing and accepting the repercussions later. We immediately have a backup plan to God's plan or his no, resulting in more debt and trouble.

What's Included in Your Credit Score?

Ironically, the number one thing God instructs us to do is the highest percentage category used when calculating your credit score. According to FICO, the top tier model used by creditors, your credit score is unique, calculated based on five categories, and only information found on your credit report. There is a misconception that you share credit scores when you're married.

There's no such thing as a joint credit report – for married couples or anyone else. Married or single, your credit report is linked to your social security number. You and your spouse may have many joint accounts if you're married, such as a mortgage, car loans, and shared credit card accounts. Those joint items will appear on both your credit reports and will affect both of your scores. Likewise, both credit scores and reports are evaluated when making combined purchases. You cannot take your spouse's credit score just because it's better. This is a good reason to discuss finances, including the five categories used to calculate your credit score.

The five categories used to calculate your credit score include the following:

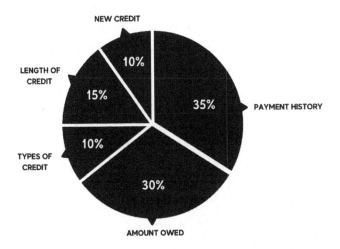

Payment History (35%) shows how well you've paid your lenders over time. This category reviews how often you've missed payments or how often payments have been late. This category should take us back to Psalms 37:21.

Amount Owed (30%) is based on the number of accounts carrying a balance, ultimately the total debt you have. If you are using a large amount of credit available to you, this could signal that you are a high-risk borrower.

Length of Credit History (15%) is a calculation showing how long your accounts have been open by using an average of all open accounts.

Credit Mix (10%) shows that if you're able to carry a mixed portfolio, you can handle different types of accounts—for example, a mortgage, auto loan, student loan, and credit card.

New Credit (10%) evaluates how often you're opening multiple accounts in a short period. Multiple inquiries on your account can negatively affect your credit.

Credit is another notch in our financial journey that requires us to obey and trust God's promises. As mentioned, God has given us heavenly instructions when it comes to debt, and your credit score and report are physical proof of your obedience to his teachings. 1 Corinthians 4:2 tells us that it is required of stewards to be found trustworthy and faithful; this includes the natural as well as the spiritual. Your spiritual account is no good if your earthly account is always in default.

CHAPTER 7: MANAGING YOUR MONEY GODS WAY

For which of you, desiring to build a tower, does not first sit down and count the cost, whether he has enough to complete it?

LUKE 14:28 (ESV)

Setting Goals–Understanding Gods Will

As a senior in high school, I remember pulling out my colored pencils and notebook and planning my life away. Boy, I was excited to get everything down on paper and even taped it to my closet door to see it every day. I wrote down my goals, how I thought life would go, who I was going to marry, where we were going to live, and everything in between. And baby, was I wrong, not about everything, but some things.

Some items I felt God on and live in the blessings and testimony of those today; however, for the others, I can now confess and say that I was operating in the flesh, and God must've stepped away for a moment while I was writing. Someone once said, if you want to make God laugh, tell Him your plans.

Contrary to what's taught in the financial sector, setting goals is your number one step to becoming financially free. Your goals represent what's important to you and the direction you're steering, pretty much like your compass. As a Christian believing in God to order your steps, you may ask, what good is it for me to set goals? Aren't I going ahead of Him? The truth is, God doesn't want us to go before Him and plan without his direction; however, He doesn't want us stagnant or sitting around just waiting on what's next. It isn't God's will for us to be in the dark about the plans He has for us. Setting goals with God will help you see what's important and the direction He's taking you.

Habakkuk 2:2-3 says, "And the Lord answered me: "Write the vision; make it plain on tablets, so he may run who reads it. For still the vision awaits its appointed time; it hastens to the end—it will not lie. If it seems slow, wait for it; it will surely come; it will not delay." As a Christian, goal setting isn't about having the exact blueprint God has for our lives but more about submitting to his leadership and what He has in store for us. What God shows us may not be for the immediate future but will be fulfilled at its appointed time.

When setting goals, your number one priority should be ensuring that God is at the center of your goals. You should pray that your goals align with the will of God and that the motivation behind your goals is pleasing to God. As you write your goals, pray Psalms 20:4, and ask God to give you the desires of your heart and make all your plans succeed. The danger in not seeking God or sitting back stems from the lack of faith and trust.

Setting goals with God shows that you trust Him in all your endeavors and on your financial journey. As you pray and are in devotion with God, seek Him for your financial goals. Allow Him to lead the conversation and show you areas you need to start saving money; car and house buying plans, and everything else. Remember not to leave anything out, no matter how small or big it may be. In your prayer time, be sure to ask God for the timing to help distinguish between short, mid, and long-term goals. Do you know that when you pray and ask God, He will give you dates, days, and times? Do not put God in a box.

Benefits of Setting Goals

- Setting goals keeps you focused and accountable
- Helps you feel accomplished
- Creates a clear plan for success
- Provides motivation for the future
- Helps trigger discipline and new behavior

Types of Goals–Short, Mid, Long Term

Through devotion with God, you're given a plan for success, and it helps trigger discipline in your prayer and personal life. Depending on what God tells you, your goals may fit into the short-, mid-, or long-term bucket.

Short-term financial goals are those goals that are completed in less than two years. Examples of short-term goals include:

- Saving for a down payment or vacation.
- Establishing an emergency fund.
- Paying off debt.

Mid-term financial goals require more money and are accomplished within two to five years. Examples of mid-term goals include:

- Paying off a large credit card balance or debt.
- Starting a business.

- Paying for a wedding.

Lastly, your long-term goals are those that require a large amount of money, planning, determination, and prayer. Funds for long-term goals should be in a high yield savings account or certificate of deposit (CDs) with a high interest rate. Examples of long-term goals include:

- Saving for a retirement fund.
- Saving for college or tuition.
- Paying off a mortgage.

* Medium and long-term savings goals can be invested in ways that will help the balance to grow over a more extended period, such as CDs, mutual funds, annuities, stocks, and bonds.

How to Set Goals

A goal-setting strategy you can apply to each goal to ensure that it can be achieved is SMART. Using the perimeters for these goals will help you succeed in any endeavor.

SPECIFIC–Make sure your goals are focused and identify a tangible outcome. Without the specifics, your goal runs the risk of being too vague to achieve, and being more specific helps you recognize what you want to achieve. Additionally, determine what resources you are going to leverage to achieve success.

Example: <u>*"I want to save money for a down payment to buy a house."*</u>

MEASURABLE–This part of the goal often answers how much or how many; it highlights how you'll achieve your goal.

Example: "I want to save <u>$6,000</u> for a down payment to buy a house."

ATTAINABLE–Although a goal is a goal, some are just easier to achieve. No matter what, your goal should be challenging but still reasonable to achieve. Reflecting on this component can reveal any potential hurdles you may discover or need to overcome to obtain success. Outline the steps you need to take to achieve your goal.

Example: "I want to save $6,000 <u>by saving $250 a month</u> for a down payment to buy a house."

RELEVANT–You've reached the moment of reality. Yes, this is the moment to pause and become truthful with yourself. Is what you're trying to achieve worthwhile to you? Is this goal aligned with your values? Do I have what it takes to achieve this goal? These types of questions help you answer the why.

Example: <u>*"Do I have an extra $250 a month to save to reach this goal?"*</u>

TIME-BOUND–Every goal needs a deadline, a target date and something that motivates you to apply the strength and discipline required to achieve your goal. This question answers "when". It's crucial to set a realistic time to achieve your goal to ensure you don't get discouraged. Setting a time that's either too short or long is not a recipe for success.

Example: "I want to save $6,000 by saving $250 a month <u>for the next 2 years (24 months)</u> for a down payment to buy a house."

REFLECTION QUESTIONS FOR EACH GOAL

1. What makes me nervous or concerned about this goal?
2. What obstacles or challenges could prevent me from reaching my goal?
3. What old habits and mindset must I get rid of to achieve this goal?
4. What can I do to feel more comfortable about this goal?

Be honest with God about what you're nervous and concerned about, and write it down for each goal. As you create each goal, design a workable plan that will enable you to begin making it a reality. Ask God to show you any obstacles or challenges that could prevent you from reaching your goal; or old habits and mindsets you must remove. Lastly, ask God what you can do to feel more confident about your plan and continue to commune with Him daily. After you set goals, it should be your mission to have several business meetings with God (as I like to call them) to ensure you're on track or not moving ahead of Him.

The key to setting goals as a Christian is leaving room for the will of God and the Holy Spirit. We may "miss the mark" at times, not because we've done something wrong, but because we'll never be on the same level as God. God is omnipresent and has the most extensive view and scope on our lives. He already knows the end from the beginning (Isaiah 46:10). I've found that the "miss" sometimes is good as it allows us to develop ourselves and trust, which ultimately becomes part of our purpose and destiny.

Lastly, we must remember to set spiritual goals in addition to financial and health goals. When spiritual goals are first, it lays the foundation for all other goals to succeed. A few examples of spiritual goals include fasting and praying regularly, being wise with your time, and prioritizing time with God. When you set and work towards achieving spiritual goals, you're more sensitive to hearing God and his plans for your life.

Budgeting

For my couples, this is when we start to hear the moans, groans, and the simple "just pray for us". Budgeting as an individual is enough work, but budgeting as a couple will either make or break you. Baby, it's not for the weak at heart or marriage.

Our responsibility is to be in covenant with God over our finances. Because of this, one of your financial goals should include creating and sticking to a budget. Do you feel like your circumstances have taken control of your financial life? Are you living paycheck to paycheck, just barely making it as long as things go well for you? What happens when the air conditioner goes out, the car breaks down, or the fridge decides to power down forever? If these inevitable financial hiccups can turn into significant crises or set you back so far that it takes forever to catch back up again, then you'll be happy to discover that life doesn't have to be this way at all!

Regardless of your income, you can take control of your financial life and look forward to a secure future. All you need is a clear plan tailored and personalized for you. When it comes to our finances, God's plan for us is to manage our finances his way. Everything we've read about is excellent; however, your budget is where the rubber meets the road. This is your way of surrendering to God and agreeing to take the steps required to complete the mission. For Christians, think of your budget as the financial stewardship tool for managing what God has allowed us to oversee. In simple terms, a budget is a process for creating a plan for your money. It helps you determine if you have or will have enough money to cover the cost. It allows you to be proactive in telling and knowing where every dollar in your household is going. Some may not believe it, but there is a sense of freedom that comes with budgeting. Until you identify problems in your spending, you're unable to walk in true healing in your finances. Budgeting allows you to put it all on paper, understanding that your financial problems don't have you but knowing you have a God who has your financial issues if you're abiding in Him. Not to be confused with deprivation, you should think of your budget as your lifestyle plan. In scripture, we find more than a few verses about the importance of budgeting:

Luke 14:28-30 (NIV) – "Suppose one of you wants to build a tower. Won't you first sit down and estimate the cost to see if you have enough money to complete it? If you lay the foundation and cannot finish it, everyone who sees it will ridicule you, saying, 'This person began to build and wasn't able to finish."

Proverbs 21:20 (NIV) – "The wise store up choice food and olive oil, but fools gulp theirs down."

Proverbs 6:6-8 (NIV)– "Go to the ant, you sluggard; consider its ways and be wise. It has no commander, no overseer or ruler, yet it stores its provisions in summer and gathers its food at harvest".

Proverbs 25:28 (KJV) – "He who has no rule over his own spirit is like a broken-down city without a wall."

1 Corinthians 16:2 (NASB) – "On the first day of every week each one of you is to put aside and save, as he may prosper so that no collections be made when I come."

When you budget, you should think of yourself as being responsible, disciplined, and disciples of Christ. You're sitting down and counting the cost to ensure you have enough money for your bills and expenses, with tithing being a top priority. We plan where each dollar goes and ultimately follow the plan. Unfortunately, there is no way to fully see the big picture of what's coming in vs. going out of your household. Spending as little as an extra $20 a day amounts to $140 a week, about $600 per month, and $7200 per year.

Another advantage of budgeting is that it allows you to ensure you're being responsible with debt and enables you to see where you can put extra towards debt to pay it off quicker. I had a beautiful 1:1 session with the amazing Tiffany "The Budgetnista" Aliche, and she reminded me that most people have 1 of 2 problems: a spend too much or a don't make enough money problem. The reality is some people have a shortage month after month, simply because they don't make enough money. Others make enough, however, fall short month after month because they're not managing it responsibly.

My favorite way to budget is to use the Zero-Based Budgeting method. With this method, every single dollar coming into the house as income is given a name. Either named a bill or expense or sent to savings. Zero-Based budgeting keeps you aware of how much money flows in and out of the household, ultimately preventing you from spending what you don't have (NerdWallet).

Budgeting is not only important because it's our tool for managing what God has given us, but it gives us control over our money; instead of our money controlling us. John Maxwell said it best when he said a budget tells your money where to go instead of wondering where it went. The worst feeling is knowing that your money is gone and not remembering where it went. It's also important because it allows you to save for expected and unexpected expenses. Being confident in your plan will also help you be confident with your decisions. As mentioned earlier, budgeting as a couple is just as important. It opens the door to you communicating with your significant about your finances. Stop what you're doing now and go ahead and schedule reoccurring monthly meetings to discuss your responsibilities and expectations.

Common Myths

A few common myths I'd like to dispel before even getting started include:

1. **Budgeting is time-consuming:** As my parents used to say, you spend your money and time on what's important to you. Changing your mindset and seeing the importance of managing your money God's way will

remove any limitations and expectations you mentally place on yourself.

2. **I've always been bad at math:** Budgeting doesn't require you to have a physics or math degree. If you can count money, you can budget. Using a template like one found on our website www.thebougiewealthgroup.com, all calculations and formulas are created for you. All you must do is enter your income, expenses, and savings goals.

3. **Budgeting will show me that I don't have any money:** You should want to confirm the truth of this statement before making assumptions. I've had clients say this, not realizing after finishing their plan that they had more than they thought. Budgeting does not equal deprivation. You should never assume that because you're budgeting, you must deprive yourself.

4. **My salary/income is too high or low:** The reality is that no matter how much money you make, a budget is needed. If you're making money, you need a budget to tell that money where it should go, no matter if it's all to savings or just a few bills.

Now that we've determined how essential using a budget is to manage our finances, you may ask, "where do I start?" It's simple and can be completed in five simple steps. Follow these easy steps to create your personalized budget and begin the process of gaining greater control over your finances:

1. **Pray to hear God's voice and better understand how you should manage your money.** Remember, God isn't a God

of lack and deprivation. He will ensure your needs and the desires of your heart are accounted for, according to his will.

2. **Identify and list all sources of net income.** The next step in deciding how to spend or save your money is to determine how much income you have coming in. Your net income is what you receive monthly after taxes. If you have an irregular pay schedule, use an estimate leaning towards the lower end. You can always increase your income once the extra pay has been confirmed; however, you should never budget for the money you don't have. Begin by listing all sources of income, including the amount and frequency that you receive your payments. Income includes any money that you receive in the form of wages or payment for work and money from irregular sources such as windfalls and inheritances.

3. **Identify and list your total expenses and bills.** Here is where you will include tithing (as a priority) at the top of all our budget templates. Determine your expenses, their type, and their frequency. It's impossible to control your expenses without first identifying them. The two most common categories of expenses are fixed and variable:

Fixed expenses reoccur on a frequent, regular basis. Your mortgage and rent payments, life, auto, health insurance premiums, and vehicle payments are fixed expenses.

Variable expenses can occur infrequently or regularly, but the amount is typically sporadic or varies. Examples of variable expenses include your monthly grocery bill, gifts, overdraft charges, and fines. These expenses are harder to estimate, but they're an essential part of a workable budget. For variable expenses, which are based on usage, use an average.

Categories to remember to include when budgeting:

- housing (rent, mortgage, lawn, security, taxes)
- utilities
- gifts (birthdays, holidays, showers, weddings)
- debt (credit cards, loans, medical)
- food (groceries, eating out, coffee)
- kids (extracurricular/sports, allowances, tuition, diapers/formula, school supplies)
- subscriptions (gym, magazine, steaming services, music, TV/cable)
- self-care (date night, grooming, books, beauty)
- medical (doctor, dentist, hospital, prescriptions, vitamins)
- for the home (cleaning supplies, paper products, furniture, décor, renovations)

4. **Plan.** Once you've identified your income and expenses, you can begin to plan how you'll spend your money and meet your financial goals.

If Income is greater than Expenses - You're in a Great position, and the remaining funds should go to savings; you want to ensure every dollar has a name.

If Expenses are greater than Income - We have a bit of an issue. You need to review your expenses, possibly decreasing the nice-to-have categories first. Additionally, this may be where additional income would help for a while.

Just as each person is unique with their talents, abilities, and preferences, their budget and financial goals are unique. Despite this, everyone can use some general rules and practices to increase their financial stability.

- In general, you'll want to save a portion of your income and use it to meet any number of common financial goals.

- Common financial goals that will increase your financial security and peace of mind include building a savings fund for emergencies, paying off debt, saving for short and long-term needs, retirement planning, investments, and so forth.

- It's essential to leave room in your budget for fun or unplanned expenses. Just like a diet to lose weight, if your plan is too strict, you are likely to cheat and not stick to it in the long term.

5. **Review.** Review your monthly statements closely the first few months to determine where adjustments are needed; repeat monthly. Identify areas of your spending that you can cut back on to fund your savings and investment plans. Also, look for ways to boost your income so you can add to your savings. By keeping your budget relevant to your current situation, you can ensure that you aren't caught unawares of changes in your income or expenses.

Saving

As much as ants aren't my favorite insect, they are the ultimate example of storing up and saving. Found in Proverbs 6:6-8, the word of God encourages us to be like the ants and not as sluggards or lazy. They were wise; even without a ruler or commander, they labored hard in the summer to gather food for the winter.

Understanding that there is a season for everything, we should always use wisdom and save for times of lack, whether expected or unexpected, to put us in a better financial position later. Not to be confused with over-saving or not lending and giving as God has instructed us to do. Sometimes we can become hoarders with our savings, not allowing us to experience the full benefits of the blessings God has for us. We find in Genesis 41 the story of Joseph and Pharoah and the importance of saving and storing enough for times of need.

In this passage, Pharoah reveals to Joseph that he has a dream, and within this dream, as he's standing by the Nile, he sees seven fat cows followed by seven skinny cows; and the skinny cows ate the fat cows. He awoke and had a very similar dream about ears of grain growing on a stalk. Joseph reveals to Pharoah that the seven fat cows and ears of grain represent seven years of plenty throughout the land of Egypt. He acknowledged that this would be followed by seven years of famine representing the skinny cows and ears of grain. Joseph advises Pharoah to store (save) during the seven years of plenty and use what was stored during the seven years of plenty for the seven years of famine.

Essentially, we find the importance of saving when things are good, not knowing when bad is coming. The 2020 pandemic proved this theory for saving in the modern day. Instead of saving for seven years, today, it's recommended to have a separate account for emergency funds; typically, between 3-6 months of your expenses.

At the end of 2019, while everyone talked about the 2020 vision, my pastor instructed his sheep to fast and seek God because something was on the horizon. However, he informed us that you didn't have to worry if you stuck with God. However, not everyone received this warning and could not predict the loss of jobs, income, and resources. Saving money shouldn't be an afterthought but should be just as important as understanding your expenses and income.

Saving will free you from various sources of stress, such as the worry that comes from living paycheck to paycheck and wondering if you have enough saved for retirement. Stressing over your lack of savings takes a toll on your physical and emotional well-being and can lead to arguments and strife with loved ones.

Saving helps you feel more secure, less stressed and can strengthen your relationships with others. If you haven't started saving for your financial goals, you aren't alone. According to Bankrate's June 2013 Financial Security Index Chart, 75% of Americans don't have enough savings to cover at least six months of their expenses, and 27% have $0 in emergency savings! The good news is that it's never too late to begin building your savings!

Ways to Save Money

- Create a budget and commit to understanding your finances.

- Identify your goals and align them with God's will for your life.

- Learn to say no

- Review areas, subscriptions, or nice to have where you can cut back

- Look for ways to reduce wasteful and unnecessary spending. Eliminate subscriptions to newspapers and magazines that you infrequently read and cut back on services for your cable TV and home telephone. Contact your carriers and seek discounts for bundled services.

- Reduce your food bill by eating at restaurants less often and eliminating fast food meals. Coffee, beverages, and most meals are nearly always less expensive when prepared from whole foods at home.

- Have faith and a plan to meet your goals

- Increasing your savings means changing your spending patterns and behavior.

- Start today! While it's never too late, the sooner you start, the longer you will have.

The Bible, The Ultimate Financial Guide

When visiting one of our favorite stores, IKEA, everything is perfect until having to get home to assemble our purchases. Although my husband thinks he can look at the picture on the front and assemble accordingly, 10 out of 10 times, he ends up praying that the instructions or guide has been included in the box. While on your financial journey, your instructions can be found in the Bible, the ultimate financial guide. God teaches us, gives us a command to be great stewards over our finances, and has given us the most incredible manual to follow. Choose today to partner with God for your next level of financial freedom. Before starting your journey, I ask that you do a few things:

1. Start with an open and prayerful mind. After all, it's about changing your mindset.

2. Ask God for forgiveness and forgive yourself for any past financial mistakes. You're starting a new journey TODAY.

3. Make notes, learn, highlight, and embrace your journey. We're breaking generational curses TODAY and learning to manage OUR finances in God's way.

4. Trust God most importantly and trust the process. With the hope that if we do as he has instructed us, the promises are great, not just on earth but also in heaven.

5. Read I Timothy 6:17-18 for divine instructions on living a healthy lifestyle.

6. Repeat after me; I AM TOO BLESSED TO BE BROKE!

APPENDIX

FINANCIAL PRAYERS

Prayer of Forgiveness

God,

I thank you for who you are to me, my family, and my friends. I know you to be Jehovah Jireh, Jehovah Rophe, Jehovah Nissi, and El Shaddai. Thank you for being a God of patience, understanding, and wisdom. Thank you that you love me so much that you've taken the time to educate me, and not only have you given me chance after chance, but you've also given instructions to help me along this journey. Lord, I repent for the financial decisions I've made resulting from the hardships I'm experiencing today for being a poor steward of the wealth assigned to me. Forgive me for not consulting with you or being sensitive to your direction. I release myself to the power of the Holy Spirit and thank you for renewing my mind. Poverty and lack will no longer define me. Now, God, I am in covenant with you, and I commit my finances to you, order my steps. Thank you for helping me steward my wealth as you've instructed and the seeds that have already been planted.

In Jesus' Name,

Amen

Prayer of Overflow

God,

Touch my heart that my giving will reflect you and only you. Please give me the wisdom to keep you at the center, use the right resources, and make the best decisions. Please help me commune with you daily, as no question, idea, request, or problem is too small or large for you. If I can think it, you can do it. As I work to attain wealth, help me that it doesn't consume me or my time. Thank you for allowing me to be a lender and not a borrower, above and not beneath. I invite you into my life and my financial journey, that I may experience miraculous streams of income, business ideas, debt and bills paid off, checks, jobs, hidden money, and expected and unexpected funds, good health, deliverance, and strength. Your word said that you would supply my needs according to your riches and glory. You even tell us that we have not because we ask not. So, God, I'm asking for an overflow in my finances and heart posture. Understanding that if I'm seeking you and managing my finances your way, then you're able to do what you do and be who you are, and that's simply God.

In Jesus' Name,

Amen

Prayer of Breakthrough & Wealth

God,

Thank you for allowing me to be generous as you've been generous with me. It is not your will for me to live in lack as I come from a royal priesthood. You will provide me with the financial resources I need. Please help me not to determine my wealth by my surroundings but by my lineage in Christ. I remove all fear of money and success, the fear of finances and having just enough. I put the mindset of poverty and lack under the blood of Jesus. I am a child of the king with many heavenly and earthly benefits and will act accordingly. I will no longer be afraid of the word budget, finances, making investments, nor of being wealthy. I will have what I need with plenty left over because I know who my father is. I'm claiming a financial breakthrough in my life right now, in Jesus' name. Help me trust you as you're leading me to wealth, not just riches. I will have everything I need when I need it, and I accept the increase. Thank you for doing the unlimited immediately. Eyes haven't seen, ears haven't heard, neither has it entered the hearts of man what you have in store for me. I am wealthy, and broke will no longer be in my vocabulary to describe my financial position. Now is my season and time, and I submit my finances to you.

In Jesus' Name,

Amen

AFFIRMATIONS

DEBT IS A THING OF
MY PAST.

MY INCOME IS
INCREASING DAILY.

MY MONEY GOALS
WILL MANIFEST
THIS YEAR.

I CONTROL MY
MONEY AND
SPENDING.

I AM WORTHY OF
MY DREAMS.

ACTUALLY, I CAN.

I AM A PERSON OF
WEALTH AND
GENEROSITY.

I AM WORTHY OF
FINANCIAL
FREEDOM.

I AM WEALTHY.

MINDSET MAKEOVER

What generational curses am I choosing to destroy by starting today?

What has the enemy told me I'll never be able to afford?

What changes will I make today to renew my mind?

SETTING FINANCIAL GOALS USING S.M.A.R.T

(S) Goal:

(M) Total Cost:

(A) Strategy:

(R) Why Is This Goal Important:

(T) Target Date:

SELF-REFLECTION QUESTIONS

1. What makes me nervous or concerned about this goal?

2. What obstacles or challenges could prevent me from reaching this goal?

3. What old habits and mindsets must i get rid of to achieve this goal?

4. What can I do to feel more confident about this goal?

Made in the USA
Columbia, SC
06 July 2022

62894631R00065